Welcome to The Spiritual Armor: Preparing for the Battle Ahead

Welcome to *The Spiritual Armor: Preparing for the Battle Ahead*, a transformative guide authored by Bishop Joshua L. Bowie, Sr., the esteemed Bishop of The Church of Foundational Truth in Humble, Texas. With over four decades of dedicated ministry, Bishop Bowie has guided his congregation through life's challenges with steadfast faith in God's Word.

Born on October 17, 1954, to Jessie Lee and Juanita Bowie, Joshua Bowie, Sr. was raised alongside six siblings: Barbara, Omis, Jesse, Oretha, Deray, Reginald, and Jeanette. His early years were marked by both triumphs and trials. At 18, Joshua felt invincible, yet by 20, he faced significant personal struggles that shaped his spiritual journey. Following an honorable discharge from the military in 1974, Bishop Bowie felt a profound call to God, leading him to seek fellowship in the Body of Christ. His spiritual journey began at the Missionary Baptist Church and was further nurtured at New Day Deliverance Holiness Church under Apostle R. Taylor, where he accepted Jesus Christ as his Lord and was filled with the Holy Ghost in 1975.

After five transformative years at New Day Deliverance, Joshua Bowie, Sr. recognized his calling to the Gospel Ministry. His passion for sharing God's Word led him to preach at open-air services and outdoor revivals, eventually becoming the Pastor of New Day Revival Center in Galveston and later in Houston. It was during his service at these churches that God revealed the vision for the Church of Foundational Truth, where he continues to serve faithfully. His commitment to ministry was further acknowledged in 2018 with an Honorary Doctorate of Divinity Degree from Gospel Ministry Outreach Theology Institution.

Bishop Bowie is blessed with the unwavering support of his wife, Lady Mary A. Bowie, to whom he has been married for nine years. Together, they have built a life and ministry rooted in faith, love, and service. They are proud parents of six children—Juanita, Josh, Roy, Lee, Engrid, and Vivian—and have grandchildren Grey, Gress, Maurizi, Little JW, Jaxon, Nathaniel, Trey, Jordan, Milan, Journey, Kayleigh, Rashawn, and Aaliyah, who continue to bring joy and inspiration to their lives.

In his daily broadcast, Bishop Bowie shares his Expository Teaching, along with Tuesday Prayer and Faith Words Wednesday, dedicated to deeper spiritual exploration and prayer. These platforms reflect his commitment to spiritual growth and community support, offering wisdom and encouragement to all who seek a closer walk with God.

The Spiritual Armor: Preparing for the Battle Ahead invites you to discover practical strategies for equipping yourself for spiritual warfare by putting on the full armor of God. This book serves as a comprehensive guide to understanding and applying each piece of spiritual armor, relying on God's strength, and standing firm in the face of life's battles.

As the first in a series of forthcoming works, this book aims to equip you with the knowledge and tools needed to prepare for and overcome spiritual challenges. By embracing the full armor of God, you can navigate the battles ahead with confidence, resilience, and faith.

Through insightful teachings, scriptural wisdom, and practical strategies, *The Spiritual Armor* is designed to inspire and support you on your journey to spiritual readiness and victory. May it guide you in preparing for the battles of life, enriching your faith, and reflecting God's strength and truth in every aspect of your life.

Table of Contents

Chapter 6: The Sword of the Spirit
- Understanding the Word of God as a Weapon
- How to Effectively Use Scripture in Spiritual Battles
- Training with the Sword of the Spirit
Chapter 7: The Power of Prayer
- The Role of Prayer in Spiritual Warfare
- Developing a Consistent Prayer Life
- Utilizing Prayer as a Weapon and Defense

Chapter 8: Standing Firm in the Strength of the Lord
- Relying on God's Strength Over Your Own
- Building Spiritual Resilience
- Encouragement and Strategies for Standing Firm

Chapter 9: Preparing for Specific Battles
- Identifying and Preparing for Personal Spiritual Challenges
- Tailoring Your Armor for Various Situations
- Case Studies and Testimonies

Chapter 10: Maintaining Your Armor
- The Importance of Regular Spiritual Maintenance
- Practices for Keeping Your Armor in Good Condition
- Continuous Growth and Readiness

Conclusion: A Life of Preparedness and Victory
- Embracing a Lifestyle of Spiritual Readiness
- Living in Victory through the Armor of God
- Final Encouragement and Reflections

Introduction: Understanding Spiritual Warfare

The Nature of Spiritual Warfare

Spiritual warfare is a deep, complex battle that extends beyond the physical realm into the spiritual dimension. This conflict involves the forces of good, represented by God and His angels, and the forces of evil, led by Satan and his demonic entities. It's a struggle that impacts every area of a believer's life, including the mental, emotional, and spiritual aspects. Understanding this battle requires recognizing that it is not merely a physical or emotional challenge but a profound spiritual conflict.

In Ephesians 6:12, Paul highlights the nature of this warfare, stating, "For we do not wrestle against flesh and blood, but against principalities, against powers, against the rulers of the darkness of this age, against spiritual hosts of wickedness in the heavenly places." This verse underscores that our struggles are not just human conflicts but are deeply spiritual, involving unseen forces working against us. The enemy, often referred to as Satan or the adversary, employs various tactics to disrupt our faith and relationship with God. These tactics can include sowing seeds of doubt, fear, and confusion, aiming to weaken our trust in God and divert us from our spiritual path.

Satan is described as a "roaring lion" in 1 Peter 5:8, emphasizing his predatory nature and the need for vigilance. Spiritual warfare is a continuous battle, where the enemy seeks to exploit our vulnerabilities and undermine our spiritual well-being. This battle can manifest in many ways, such as through personal challenges, temptations, and spiritual attacks. Recognizing these manifestations helps believers stay alert and prepared to confront them.

The nature of spiritual warfare also involves understanding that it affects all areas of our lives. Mental struggles, such as persistent doubts or negative thoughts, can be seen as battlegrounds where the enemy tries to gain a foothold. Emotional struggles, such as anxiety or depression, can also be linked to spiritual attacks aimed at disrupting our peace and joy. By understanding this interconnectedness, believers can better prepare themselves to face these challenges with a spiritual mindset.

The Importance of Being Prepared

Preparation is crucial in spiritual warfare as it equips believers to face the enemy's attacks with strength and confidence. Without proper preparation, believers may find themselves vulnerable and unprepared for the challenges they encounter.

Preparation starts with awareness and vigilance. Many believers may not fully recognize the subtle ways in which spiritual attacks can manifest, making them more susceptible to being caught off guard. Being aware of the signs of spiritual opposition—such as feelings of overwhelming doubt, sudden conflicts, or emotional turmoil—helps believers stay proactive in their spiritual lives and respond effectively to these challenges.

Equipping oneself with the spiritual resources provided by God is another essential aspect of preparation. Ephesians 6:10-18 outlines the armor of God, which includes the belt of truth, breastplate of righteousness, shoes of the gospel of peace, shield of faith, helmet of salvation, and sword of the Spirit. Each piece of this armor serves a specific purpose in protecting and empowering believers in their spiritual battles. Understanding and applying these elements in daily life is vital for standing firm against the schemes of the devil.

The belt of truth is foundational, representing the importance of embracing and living out God's truth. It secures and supports the other pieces of armor, providing stability and preventing deception. The breastplate of righteousness protects the heart and vital organs, symbolizing the importance of living a righteous life and being covered by the righteousness of Christ. The shoes of the gospel of peace ensure stability and readiness, grounding believers in Christ's peace and preparing them to share the gospel with others.

The shield of faith is crucial for defense, extinguishing the fiery darts of doubt and fear that the enemy throws. Faith acts as a barrier against the enemy's attacks and allows believers to remain steadfast in their trust in God. The helmet of salvation protects the mind, focusing on the assurance and security of salvation in Christ. It helps believers resist doubts and maintain clarity in their spiritual journey. The sword of the Spirit, which is the Word of God, is the only offensive weapon in the armor. It provides guidance and defense against deception, helping believers to counter the enemy's lies effectively.

Preparation also involves cultivating a strong prayer life. Prayer is a powerful tool in spiritual warfare, connecting believers with God's power and intervention. Ephesians 6:18 emphasizes the importance of prayer, stating, "Praying always with all prayer and supplication in the Spirit." Regular and heartfelt prayer helps believers seek God's guidance, strength, and protection, enabling them to face spiritual challenges with confidence.

Additionally, preparation includes ongoing spiritual growth and maturity. Spiritual growth involves studying the Bible, developing a deeper relationship with God, and growing in faith. As believers mature spiritually, they become better equipped to handle the complexities of spiritual warfare. Growth in wisdom, discernment, and resilience enables believers to navigate spiritual battles with greater effectiveness.

Dependence on God's strength and resources is a key element of preparation. Spiritual warfare is not a battle that can be fought on human strength alone; it requires reliance on God's power and provisions. By acknowledging that ultimate victory comes from God, believers can face spiritual battles with assurance and hope, knowing that God's strength is sufficient for every challenge they encounter.

Overview of the Armor of God

The armor of God, as described in Ephesians 6:10-18, is a comprehensive set of spiritual tools designed to protect and empower believers in their spiritual battles:

1   **The Belt of Truth**: The belt of truth is foundational, representing the importance of living by God's truth. Just as a physical belt secures and supports armor, the truth of God's Word secures and stabilizes the believer's entire spiritual armor. Embracing and living out this truth prevents deception and provides clarity in spiritual battles.

2   **The Breastplate of Righteousness**: This piece of armor protects the heart and vital organs, symbolizing the importance of living in accordance with God's standards. The breastplate of righteousness represents maintaining a right

relationship with God and living a life of integrity. It shields believers from accusations and attacks aimed at undermining their spiritual standing.

3   **The Shoes of the Gospel of Peace**: The shoes of the gospel of peace represent readiness and stability. In Roman armor, shoes provided mobility and support, similar to how the gospel of peace grounds believers and prepares them to share the message of Christ. These shoes symbolize the grounding in Christ's peace and the readiness to spread the gospel.

4   **The Shield of Faith**: The shield of faith is essential for protection against the enemy's fiery darts — attacks that seek to ignite doubts and fears. Faith is the assurance of things hoped for and the conviction of things not seen (Hebrews 11:1). The shield of faith enables believers to extinguish these fiery darts and remain steadfast in their trust in God's promises.

5   **The Helmet of Salvation**: The helmet of salvation protects the mind, which is often a battleground for spiritual attacks. Salvation represents the deliverance and security believers have in Christ. The helmet of salvation helps believers focus on their identity in Christ and the security of their salvation, protecting their minds from doubts and fears.

6   **The Sword of the Spirit**: The sword of the Spirit, which is the Word of God, is the only offensive weapon in the armor of God. It represents the power of Scripture to counter and defeat the enemy's lies and temptations. Effective use of the sword of the Spirit involves knowing and applying Scripture to combat spiritual attacks and guide one's actions.

Ephesians 6:18 further emphasizes the importance of prayer in spiritual warfare. Prayer connects believers with God's power and enables them to seek His guidance and intervention. By understanding and utilizing the armor of God, believers can stand firm against spiritual attacks and live a victorious Christian life.

In summary, spiritual warfare involves understanding the nature of the conflict, preparing oneself through awareness, spiritual resources, and prayer, and utilizing the armor of God to navigate the battles faced. The armor equips believers to confront spiritual challenges with strength and resilience, ensuring they can achieve victory in Christ.

Chapter 1:

The Belt of Truth

The Role of Truth in Spiritual Warfare

In the realm of spiritual warfare, truth plays a foundational and critical role. The Belt of Truth, as described in Ephesians 6:14, is the first piece of the armor of God, highlighting its importance in the believer's spiritual protection and readiness. Truth is not just a passive concept but an active force that shapes and sustains the entire armor of God.

Truth is essential in spiritual warfare because it serves as the anchor and stabilizer for everything else. Just as a physical belt holds together and supports the rest of the soldier's armor, the Belt of Truth secures and supports the believer's spiritual defense. Without truth, the rest of the armor is compromised, and the believer's position becomes unstable.

In John 8:32, Jesus says, "You shall know the truth, and the truth shall make you free." This verse emphasizes that truth liberates and empowers believers. Knowing and embracing God's truth is crucial for recognizing and resisting the enemy's lies and deceptions. Satan, the father of lies (John 8:44), constantly seeks to distort, obscure, or outright deny the truth to undermine the believer's faith. The Belt of Truth, therefore, acts as a defense against these deceitful tactics, providing clarity and stability in the midst of spiritual battles.

The importance of truth extends beyond mere intellectual acknowledgment. It involves a deep, personal engagement with God's truth, allowing it to permeate every aspect of life. Truth is not only about knowing what is right but also about living it out consistently. This integration of truth into daily life fortifies believers against the enemy's schemes and strengthens their spiritual resilience.

How to Embrace and Live Out Truth

Embracing and living out truth requires a deliberate and intentional approach. It begins with a commitment to understanding and internalizing God's Word. The Bible, as the ultimate source of truth, provides the foundation upon which believers build their lives. Engaging with Scripture through regular reading, study, and meditation helps believers gain insight into God's truth and apply it to their lives.

1   **Study and Meditate on Scripture**: Regular engagement with the Bible is crucial for understanding and embracing truth. Study involves not only reading but also interpreting and applying biblical principles. Meditation allows believers to reflect deeply on God's Word, helping them internalize and live out its teachings. By immersing oneself in Scripture, believers can build a strong foundation of truth that guides their thoughts, actions, and decisions.

2   **Align Your Life with Biblical Truth**: Embracing truth means aligning one's life with the teachings of Scripture. This involves evaluating personal beliefs, attitudes, and behaviors in light of God's Word and making necessary adjustments. It requires honesty and self-reflection, acknowledging areas where one may be deviating from God's truth and taking steps to correct those deviations. Living in accordance with biblical truth involves integrity, consistency, and a commitment to righteousness.

3   **Cultivate a Relationship with God**: Embracing truth also involves developing a personal relationship with God. Through prayer, worship, and fellowship, believers deepen their understanding of God's character and His truth. A close relationship with God enhances discernment and helps believers remain steadfast in their commitment to truth. It provides guidance and strength to resist temptation and stand firm in the face of spiritual challenges.

4   **Practice Truthfulness in Relationships**: Living out truth involves being truthful in all relationships. Honesty and transparency are crucial in fostering trust and integrity in interpersonal interactions. By practicing truthfulness, believers reflect God's character and build stronger, more authentic relationships. This commitment to truth in relationships also serves as a testimony to others of God's transformative power.

Practical Steps for Wearing the Belt of Truth

Wearing the Belt of Truth involves practical actions that incorporate God's truth into daily life. These steps help believers effectively utilize this piece of spiritual armor and maintain their spiritual readiness.

1   **Daily Scripture Reading and Meditation**: Establish a routine for reading and meditating on Scripture. Choose a specific time each day to engage with God's Word, whether through personal study, devotional materials, or Bible study groups. Reflect on passages that speak to the challenges you face and seek to apply their truths to your life.

2   **Commit to Personal Integrity**: Evaluate your life for areas where you may not be living in alignment with God's truth. This may involve confessing and repenting of sin, making amends in relationships, or changing habits that conflict with biblical teachings. Strive to maintain honesty and integrity in all aspects of life, ensuring that your actions align with the truth you profess.

3   **Seek Accountability and Support**: Surround yourself with fellow believers who can provide support, encouragement, and accountability. Engage in fellowship and discussions that promote spiritual growth and mutual encouragement. Having a network of trusted individuals can help you stay committed to living out God's truth and provide guidance when facing challenges.

4   **Equip Yourself with Truth in Decision-Making**: When faced with decisions, evaluate them through the lens of biblical truth. Consider how your choices align with God's Word and seek wisdom through prayer and consultation with spiritual mentors. Ensuring that your decisions are grounded in truth helps maintain consistency and integrity in your life.

5   **Use Scripture in Spiritual Battles**: When confronted with spiritual attacks or doubts, counter them with Scripture. Memorize key verses that address common temptations or struggles and use them as a defense against the enemy's lies. Applying God's truth in these situations helps reinforce your spiritual armor and strengthens your ability to resist.

6   **Reflect on God's Promises**: Embrace and meditate on the promises of God found in Scripture. These promises provide assurance and encouragement in the face of adversity. Reflecting on God's promises helps reinforce your trust in His truth and strengthens your confidence in His ability to fulfill His Word.

7   **Share Truth with Others**: Engage in conversations about God's truth with others, whether through personal interactions or broader outreach efforts. Sharing the truth of the gospel and biblical principles with others not only fulfills the Great Commission but also reinforces your own understanding and commitment to truth.

By following these practical steps, believers can effectively wear the Belt of Truth and remain steadfast in their spiritual battles. Embracing and living out truth requires ongoing effort and dedication, but it provides essential protection and stability in the face of spiritual challenges. As the foundational piece of spiritual armor, the Belt of Truth secures and supports the entire armor, enabling believers to stand firm and resist the enemy's attacks with confidence and clarity.

Chapter 2:

The Breastplate of Righteousness

The Significance of Righteousness

In the metaphorical armor of God described in Ephesians 6:14, the Breastplate of Righteousness is a crucial piece that protects vital areas of the believer's spiritual life. Just as a physical breastplate shields the chest and vital organs of a soldier, the Breastplate of Righteousness safeguards the believer's heart and character from the attacks of the enemy.

Righteousness, in biblical terms, refers to a state of being right or just according to God's standards. It encompasses both the imputed righteousness of Christ and the practical righteousness that believers are called to live out in their daily lives. The significance of righteousness in spiritual warfare lies in its role as a protective shield that guards against the enemy's schemes and maintains the integrity of the believer's relationship with God.

In 2 Corinthians 5:21, the Apostle Paul writes, "For our sake, he made him to be sin who knew no sin, so that in him we might become the righteousness of God." This verse highlights the foundational aspect of righteousness—Christ's sacrificial work on the cross provides believers with His righteousness, enabling them to stand before God justified and clean. This imputed righteousness is the starting point of the believer's spiritual armor.

However, righteousness is not limited to the positional aspect provided by Christ. It also involves the practical outworking of that righteousness in daily living. Philippians 2:15 calls believers to be "blameless and innocent, children of God without blemish in the midst of a crooked and twisted generation." This call to practical righteousness involves living in a manner that reflects God's character and upholds His standards.

The Breastplate of Righteousness is essential for several reasons. Firstly, it protects the heart, symbolizing the center of a person's emotional and moral life. The enemy often targets the heart with temptations, doubts, and accusations, seeking to undermine the believer's integrity and trust in God. Righteousness acts as a shield that deflects these attacks and maintains the believer's spiritual vitality.

Secondly, righteousness enhances the believer's testimony and witness. When believers live out practical righteousness, they reflect God's character and attract others to the truth of the gospel. A life marked by righteousness serves as a powerful witness to the transformative power of Christ and draws others to seek the same transformation.

Developing a Righteous Heart

Developing a righteous heart involves embracing the righteousness provided by Christ and actively pursuing a life that reflects God's standards. This process requires intentional effort and a willingness to cooperate with the work of the Holy Spirit.

1   **Embrace Christ's Righteousness**: The foundation of righteousness is the imputed righteousness of Christ. Believers must accept and understand that their standing before God is based on Christ's righteousness rather than their own merits. This understanding provides a secure basis for spiritual growth and empowers believers to pursue practical righteousness. Romans 5:1 states, "Therefore, since we have been justified by faith, we have peace with God through our Lord Jesus Christ." Embracing this truth helps believers approach God with confidence and receive His grace for daily living.

2   **Pursue Personal Holiness**: Practical righteousness involves actively pursuing a life of holiness and obedience to God's commands. This pursuit requires a conscious effort to align one's thoughts, actions, and attitudes with biblical principles. 1 Peter 1:15-16 exhorts believers to "be holy in all your conduct, since it is written, 'You shall be holy, for I am holy.'" Developing a righteous heart involves a daily commitment to living in accordance with God's Word and reflecting His character in all areas of life.

3   **Cultivate a Relationship with God**: A righteous heart is nurtured through a deep and personal relationship with God. Prayer, worship, and regular engagement with Scripture foster spiritual growth and enable believers to discern and follow God's will. James 4:8

encourages believers to "draw near to God, and he will draw near to you." Cultivating this relationship strengthens the believer's resolve to live righteously and provides the necessary spiritual nourishment for maintaining a pure heart.

4   **Seek Accountability and Growth**: Developing a righteous heart involves seeking accountability and support from fellow believers. Engaging in fellowship, participating in Bible studies, and receiving guidance from spiritual mentors contribute to spiritual growth and accountability. Proverbs 27:17 states, "Iron sharpens iron, and one man sharpens another." Being part of a supportive community helps believers stay committed to righteousness and provides encouragement in the journey of spiritual development.

5   **Practice Confession and Repentance**: Maintaining a righteous heart requires ongoing confession and repentance. Regularly acknowledging and repenting of sin restores the believer's fellowship with God and ensures that the heart remains pure. 1 John 1:9 promises, "If we confess our sins, he is faithful and just to forgive us our sins and to cleanse us from all unrighteousness." Practicing confession and repentance helps believers stay aligned with God's standards and reinforces their commitment to living righteously.

How to Protect Yourself with the Breastplate of Righteousness

Wearing the Breastplate of Righteousness involves practical steps that integrate righteousness into everyday life. These steps help believers protect themselves from spiritual attacks and maintain their integrity in the face of challenges.

1   **Guard Your Heart**: The Breastplate of Righteousness protects the heart, symbolizing the center of a person's moral and emotional life. To guard the heart, believers should be vigilant about what they allow to influence their thoughts and emotions. Philippians 4:8 provides guidance: "Finally, brothers, whatever is true, whatever is honorable, whatever is just, whatever is pure, whatever is lovely, whatever is commendable—if there is any excellence, if there is anything worthy of praise, think about these things." By focusing on positive and righteous influences, believers can safeguard their hearts from negative or corrupting influences.

14

2   **Live with Integrity**: Practical righteousness involves living with integrity and consistency. Believers should strive to align their actions with their professed beliefs and ensure that their conduct reflects God's standards. Colossians 3:23 encourages believers to "work heartily, as for the Lord and not for men." Living with integrity means conducting oneself with honesty, fairness, and purity in all interactions, whether personal, professional, or relational.

3   **Equip Yourself with Scripture**: The Word of God serves as a powerful tool for protecting oneself with the Breastplate of Righteousness. By studying and memorizing Scripture, believers can strengthen their understanding of God's standards and be better prepared to resist temptation and deception. Psalm 119:11 states, "I have stored up your word in my heart, that I might not sin against you." Equipping oneself with Scripture enhances the ability to make righteous choices and withstand spiritual attacks.

4   **Commit to Accountability**: Engaging in accountability relationships with fellow believers provides an additional layer of protection. Being open and honest with trusted individuals about struggles and challenges helps maintain accountability and reinforces the commitment to righteousness. Ecclesiastes 4:9-10 highlights the value of accountability: "Two are better than one... For if they fall, one will lift up his fellow." Having a support system helps believers stay accountable and provides encouragement in their pursuit of righteousness.

5   **Pray for Strength and Guidance**: Prayer is a vital component of protecting oneself with the Breastplate of Righteousness. Seeking God's strength and guidance through prayer helps believers remain steadfast in their commitment to righteousness. Ephesians 6:18 instructs believers to "pray at all times in the Spirit, with all prayer and supplication." Prayer fortifies the believer's spiritual armor, providing the necessary strength and wisdom to navigate challenges and uphold righteousness.

By following these practical steps, believers can wear the Breastplate of Righteousness effectively and guard against spiritual attacks. Developing a righteous heart and living out practical righteousness require ongoing effort but offer essential protection and stability in spiritual challenges. The Breastplate of Righteousness is a crucial piece of God's armor, safeguarding the believer's heart and ensuring a resilient spiritual life.

Chapter 3:

The Shoes of the Gospel of Peace

The Peace of the Gospel as a Foundation

In Ephesians 6:15, Paul instructs believers to "have your feet shod with the preparation of the gospel of peace." This piece of spiritual armor symbolizes the stability and readiness that comes from embracing and spreading the peace offered through the gospel of Jesus Christ. Just as shoes provide stability and protection for the feet, the gospel of peace equips believers with the foundation needed to navigate life's challenges and engage in spiritual warfare.

The peace of the gospel is not merely the absence of conflict but a profound, enduring tranquility that arises from a restored relationship with God through Jesus Christ. This peace, often referred to as "peace with God" (Romans 5:1) and "the peace of God" (Philippians 4:7), is foundational for a victorious Christian life. It provides believers with the assurance that they are reconciled with God and secure in their salvation, enabling them to face trials with confidence and stability.

The Peace of God is a deep-seated tranquility that transcends circumstances. Philippians 4:7 describes it as a peace that "surpasses all understanding." This peace guards the heart and mind of believers, providing comfort and assurance in the midst of life's uncertainties and difficulties. It is not dependent on external factors but is rooted in the relationship believers have with God through Christ.

Peace with God refers to the reconciliation achieved through Christ's sacrifice. Romans 5:1 states, "Since we have been justified by faith, we have peace with God through our Lord Jesus Christ." This peace signifies the end of the enmity between humanity and God, made possible by Jesus' atoning work. It establishes a secure foundation for believers, knowing that they are forgiven and accepted by God, which in turn impacts how they approach and respond to life's challenges.

The shoes of the gospel of peace are vital for spiritual warfare as they provide the stability and readiness needed to advance in faith. They allow believers to stand firm and move forward with confidence, knowing that their spiritual footing is secure. This peace equips them to handle conflicts and trials with a calm assurance and to be effective witnesses of Christ's message of reconciliation and hope.

How to Share and Live the Gospel Daily

Living out and sharing the gospel of peace involves integrating its principles into everyday life and actively proclaiming its message to others. This daily practice ensures that the peace of the gospel is not just a theoretical concept but a tangible reality that influences every aspect of a believer's life.

1 **Embrace the Gospel's Peace in Your Life**: To share the gospel effectively, one must first fully embrace its peace in their own life. This involves experiencing the transformative power of the gospel and allowing it to shape one's attitudes, actions, and relationships. John 14:27 records Jesus saying, "Peace I leave with you; my peace I give to you." Embracing this peace means allowing it to permeate your thoughts, emotions, and interactions with others. By living in the reality of this peace, you become a living testament to the gospel's power.

2 **Practice Forgiveness and Reconciliation**: Living out the gospel of peace requires practicing forgiveness and reconciliation in relationships. Colossians 3:13 instructs believers to "bear with one another and, if one has a complaint against another, forgive each other; as the Lord has forgiven you, so you also must forgive." This practice of extending grace and seeking resolution in conflicts reflects the gospel's message and demonstrates the peace it brings. By modeling forgiveness and reconciliation, you make the gospel's peace visible to others.

3 **Promote Unity and Understanding**: The gospel of peace calls believers to promote unity and understanding within the body of Christ and beyond. Ephesians 4:3 encourages believers to "be eager to maintain the unity of the Spirit in the bond of peace." This involves actively seeking to understand and appreciate others' perspectives, fostering an environment of mutual respect and harmony. Promoting unity and

understanding aligns with the gospel's message and creates an atmosphere where the peace of Christ can flourish.

4   **Proclaim the Gospel's Message**: Sharing the gospel involves proclaiming the message of peace to those who have not yet heard it. This can be done through personal conversations, evangelistic efforts, and living a life that reflects the gospel's values. Romans 10:15 states, "How beautiful are the feet of those who preach the good news!" Proclaiming the gospel involves more than words; it requires living out the message and being a witness of Christ's love and peace.

5   **Seek Opportunities for Outreach**: Actively seeking opportunities for outreach and service enables believers to share the gospel of peace in practical ways. This may involve engaging in community service, supporting missions, or reaching out to those in need. Matthew 5:14-16 calls believers to be "the light of the world" and "a city set on a hill." By seeking opportunities to serve and share, believers can extend the peace of the gospel to others and make a tangible impact in their communities.

Equipping Yourself with the Shoes of Peace

Equipping oneself with the shoes of peace involves practical steps to ensure that you are ready to stand firm and advance in your faith. These steps help believers maintain their spiritual stability and effectively share the gospel message.

1   **Regular Prayer and Reflection**: Regular prayer and reflection are essential for maintaining the peace of the gospel. Prayer connects believers with God and provides a space for seeking His guidance, strength, and peace. Philippians 4:6-7 encourages believers to "pray about everything" and promises that the peace of God will guard their hearts and minds. Regular prayer and reflection help believers stay grounded in the peace of the gospel and navigate challenges with confidence.

2   **Study and Meditate on Scripture**: Studying and meditating on Scripture reinforces the truth of the gospel and strengthens the foundation of peace. Psalm 119:105 states, "Your word is a lamp to my feet and a light to my path." By immersing oneself in the Word of God, believers gain insight into God's promises and His plan for their lives. This knowledge equips them with the spiritual stability needed to navigate life's challenges and share the gospel effectively.

3   **Build a Supportive Community**: Being part of a supportive Christian community provides encouragement and accountability in living out the gospel of peace. Hebrews 10:24-25 emphasizes the importance of "considering how to stir up one another to love and good works" and "not neglecting to meet together." Engaging in fellowship and mutual support helps believers remain steadfast in their commitment to peace and strengthens their ability to share the gospel.

4   **Develop Resilience and Perseverance**: Equipping oneself with the shoes of peace requires developing resilience and perseverance in the face of trials. James 1:2-4 encourages believers to "count it all joy" when facing trials, knowing that such tests produce endurance and strengthen faith. Building resilience helps believers maintain their spiritual stability and continue advancing in their faith, even when faced with challenges and obstacles.

5   **Practice Daily Application**: Applying the principles of the gospel of peace in daily life ensures that it remains a practical and lived reality. This involves making choices that reflect the peace of Christ, such as responding with grace in difficult situations, seeking reconciliation in conflicts, and living with a mindset of love and forgiveness. By practicing daily application, believers integrate the peace of the gospel into their lives and become effective witnesses to its transformative power.

By following these practical steps, believers can effectively equip themselves with the shoes of the gospel of peace. Embracing and living out the peace of the gospel provides stability and readiness for spiritual challenges and opportunities. As believers stand firm in this peace and actively share it with others, they fulfill their calling to advance the message of reconciliation and hope, reflecting the transformative power of Christ in their lives and communities.

Chapter 4:

The Shield of Faith

The Power of Faith in Battle

In Ephesians 6:16, Paul emphasizes the importance of the shield of faith, saying, "In addition to all this, take up the shield of faith, with which you can extinguish all the flaming arrows of the evil one." This powerful metaphor underscores faith's critical role in spiritual warfare. Just as a physical shield offers protection from physical attacks, the shield of faith serves as a defensive tool against the fiery darts of doubt, fear, and temptation that the enemy hurls at believers.

Faith is not just a passive belief but an active, dynamic force that protects and sustains believers in their spiritual journey. It is a deep trust in God's promises and His character, allowing believers to stand firm against the trials and tribulations that come their way. The power of faith lies in its ability to provide a sense of assurance and confidence in God's sovereignty and goodness, even when circumstances are challenging or unclear.

In spiritual battles, the shield of faith acts as a protective barrier, intercepting and neutralizing the attacks of the enemy. These attacks can take many forms, including doubts about God's promises, fears about the future, or temptations to stray from God's path. Faith, when firmly established, repels these attacks and maintains spiritual stability. It is not merely about believing in God but trusting Him to fulfill His promises and deliver on His word, regardless of the situation.

Strengthening Your Faith in Challenging Times

Strengthening your faith, especially in challenging times, is crucial for effectively using the shield of faith. Developing a robust faith involves intentional practices and attitudes that deepen your trust in God and

His promises. Here are some strategies to help fortify your faith:

1. **Immerse Yourself in Scripture**: The Bible is the primary source of knowledge about God's promises and His faithfulness. Regular reading and meditation on Scripture build a strong foundation of faith. Romans 10:17 states, "So faith comes from hearing, and hearing through the word of Christ." By immersing yourself in God's Word, you reinforce your understanding of His character and promises, which strengthens your faith. Reflect on passages that highlight God's faithfulness, His provision, and His love.

2. **Pray Continuously**: Prayer is a vital practice for nurturing and reinforcing faith. Through prayer, you communicate with God, seek His guidance, and express your trust in His plan. Philippians 4:6-7 encourages believers to "present your requests to God" and promises that "the peace of God, which transcends all understanding, will guard your hearts and your minds in Christ Jesus." Regular prayer helps you stay connected to God and reinforces your reliance on Him.

3. **Reflect on Past Victories**: Remembering and reflecting on past experiences where God has proven Himself faithful can bolster your faith. By recounting how God has previously provided, protected, or guided you, you build confidence in His continued faithfulness. This practice involves keeping a journal or making mental notes of instances where God's hand was evident in your life. Reflecting on these moments reinforces your trust in His ability to handle current and future challenges.

4. **Seek Fellowship and Encouragement**: Surrounding yourself with a supportive community of believers can significantly impact your faith. Hebrews 10:24-25 encourages believers to "consider how to stir up one another to love and good works" and "not neglect to meet together." Engaging with fellow Christians provides encouragement, support, and accountability, helping you maintain and strengthen your faith. Share your struggles and victories with others who can offer prayer, advice, and perspective.

5   Practice Gratitude: Cultivating a heart of gratitude helps maintain a positive outlook and reinforces faith. By focusing on the blessings and provisions you have received, you shift your perspective from what is lacking to what has been provided. 1 Thessalonians 5:18 instructs believers to "give thanks in all circumstances." Practicing gratitude acknowledges God's goodness and reinforces your trust in His ongoing care and provision.

6   Engage in Worship and Praise: Worship and praise are powerful ways to strengthen faith. Singing songs of worship, expressing adoration, and acknowledging God's greatness shift your focus from challenges to God's majesty and power. Psalm 34:1 says, "I will bless the Lord at all times; His praise shall continually be in my mouth." Engaging in worship helps you connect with God and renews your sense of trust and confidence in Him.

Using the Shield of Faith to Defend Against Doubts and Attacks

The shield of faith is designed to protect believers from the various attacks of the enemy. These attacks can manifest as doubts, fears, and temptations. Knowing how to effectively use the shield of faith involves understanding these attacks and applying faith to counteract them.

1   Addressing Doubts: Doubts can undermine faith and create vulnerabilities in the spiritual armor. When faced with doubts, use the shield of faith to counteract them by reminding yourself of God's promises and past faithfulness. James 1:6 encourages believers to "ask in faith with no doubting," as doubting can lead to instability. Address doubts by recalling specific promises from Scripture, seeking answers through prayer and study, and remembering past experiences of God's faithfulness.

2   Counteracting Fear: Fear is another common attack that can undermine faith and create a sense of helplessness. To defend against fear, apply the shield of faith by focusing on God's sovereignty and His ability to handle every situation. 2

Timothy 1:7 states, "For God gave us a spirit not of fear but of power and love and self-control." By trusting in God's control and His promises of protection, you can combat fear and maintain spiritual stability.

3 **Resisting Temptations**: Temptations are designed to lure believers away from God's path and into sin. The shield of faith helps resist these temptations by reinforcing your commitment to God's standards and promises. 1 Corinthians 10:13 promises that "God is faithful, and He will not let you be tempted beyond your ability." By trusting in this promise and relying on God's strength, you can resist temptations and stay true to your faith.

4 **Maintaining Confidence**: The shield of faith helps maintain confidence in God's plan and purpose, even when circumstances seem unfavorable. Hebrews 11:1 defines faith as "the assurance of things hoped for, the conviction of things not seen." By holding firmly to this assurance, you can face challenges with confidence, knowing that God is working all things for your good.

5 **Building Spiritual Resilience**: Using the shield of faith involves developing spiritual resilience, the ability to bounce back from setbacks and remain steadfast in faith. This resilience is built through continuous prayer, Scripture study, and reliance on God's promises. Romans 5:3-4 explains that suffering produces endurance, and endurance produces character, and character produces hope. By building resilience, you strengthen your ability to use the shield of faith effectively in spiritual battles.

In conclusion, the shield of faith is an essential component of the armor of God, offering protection against the attacks of doubt, fear, and temptation. By actively engaging in practices that strengthen your faith and applying it to counteract these attacks, you can maintain spiritual stability and confidence. Embracing the power of faith and utilizing it as a shield ensures that you are well-equipped to face the challenges of spiritual warfare and remain steadfast in your journey with God.

Chapter 5:

The Helmet of Salvation

The Assurance of Salvation

The helmet of salvation is a vital piece of spiritual armor mentioned in Ephesians 6:17, where Paul instructs believers to "take the helmet of salvation." In the context of spiritual warfare, this helmet symbolizes the protection that salvation provides to our minds and hearts. To fully grasp the significance of the helmet of salvation, it's essential to understand the assurance of salvation and its profound impact on our spiritual lives.

The Nature of Salvation

Salvation, in Christian theology, refers to the deliverance from sin and its consequences, achieved through faith in Jesus Christ. It encompasses forgiveness of sins, reconciliation with God, and the promise of eternal life. This comprehensive understanding of salvation involves several key components:

1 **Forgiveness of Sin**: Central to salvation is the forgiveness of sin. Romans 3:23-24 states, "For all have sinned and fall short of the glory of God, and are justified by his grace as a gift, through the redemption that is in Christ Jesus." Through Christ's sacrificial death and resurrection, believers are granted forgiveness and released from the penalty of sin.

2 **Reconciliation with God**: Salvation restores the broken relationship between humanity and God. 2 Corinthians 5:18 affirms, "All this is from God, who through Christ reconciled us to himself and gave us the ministry of reconciliation." Through salvation, believers are brought into a right relationship with God, overcoming the separation caused by

sin.

3   **Eternal Life**: Salvation includes the promise of eternal life
with God. John 3:16 proclaims, "For God so loved the world,
that he gave his only Son, that whoever believes in him should
not perish but have eternal life." This promise assures
believers of a future where they will dwell in the presence of
God forever.

The Assurance of Salvation

The assurance of salvation is the confidence that believers have in
their eternal security and relationship with God. This assurance is
crucial for maintaining spiritual strength and resilience. Here's how
believers can experience and strengthen their assurance of salvation:

1   **Understanding the Basis of Assurance**: Assurance of
salvation is grounded in the promises of God, not in our own
efforts or feelings. 1 John 5:13 states, "I write these things to
you who believe in the name of the Son of God that you may
know that you have eternal life." This knowledge is based on
the truth of God's Word and His unchanging promises, rather
than our fluctuating emotions or performance.

2   **Faith in Christ's Work**: Assurance is rooted in faith in the
finished work of Christ. Ephesians 2:8-9 emphasizes that "by
grace you have been saved through faith. And this is not your
own doing; it is the gift of God, not a result of works, so that
no one may boast." Believers can be assured of their salvation
because it is a gift from God, secured by Christ's sacrifice, not
by human effort.

3   **Evidence of Salvation**: While assurance is based on faith, it is
also evidenced by a transformed life. 2 Corinthians 5:17
explains, "Therefore, if anyone is in Christ, he is a new
creation. The old has passed away; behold, the new has come."
The presence of spiritual fruit and a desire to follow Christ are
indicators of genuine salvation and contribute to the

confidence that one is secure in Christ.

4   **Personal Relationship with God**: Assurance is also enhanced
    through a personal relationship with God. Regular prayer,
    worship, and engagement with Scripture strengthen this
    relationship and reaffirm the believer's identity as a child of
    God. Romans 8:16 declares, "The Spirit himself bears witness
    with our spirit that we are children of God." The inner witness
    of the Holy Spirit provides reassurance of our standing before
    God.

Guarding Your Mind and Thoughts

The helmet of salvation plays a crucial role in guarding the mind and
thoughts, which are often targets of spiritual attack. Our thoughts and
mental state significantly impact our spiritual well-being and
effectiveness in battle. Here's how the helmet of salvation helps
protect the mind:

1   **Protection Against Doubts**: Doubts about salvation and
    God's promises can undermine spiritual stability. The helmet
    of salvation provides protection by reinforcing the certainty of
    salvation. By anchoring your thoughts in the assurance of
    God's promises and the truth of Scripture, you can guard
    against the doubts that the enemy may sow. Ephesians 6:17
    describes salvation as a helmet that shields our minds from
    such attacks.

2   **Renewing the Mind**: Romans 12:2 instructs believers to "be
    transformed by the renewal of your mind." The helmet of
    salvation facilitates this renewal by aligning thoughts with
    God's truth. This involves rejecting worldly influences and
    embracing the truth of Scripture. By meditating on God's
    Word and allowing it to shape your thoughts, you can protect
    your mind from negative or harmful thinking.

3   **Guarding Against Temptations**: The mind is often a

battleground for temptations and sinful desires. The helmet of salvation helps protect against these temptations by reinforcing the believer's identity in Christ and the commitment to live according to His standards. Colossians 3:2 advises believers to "set your minds on things that are above, not on things that are on earth." By focusing on heavenly things and the truths of salvation, you can resist temptations and maintain spiritual integrity.

4   **Maintaining Peace**: The helmet of salvation also contributes to maintaining inner peace. Philippians 4:7 promises that "the peace of God, which surpasses all understanding, will guard your hearts and your minds in Christ Jesus." This peace, rooted in the assurance of salvation, helps protect against anxiety and mental unrest. By anchoring your thoughts in the certainty of God's salvation, you can experience peace even in challenging circumstances.

Embracing the Helmet of Salvation for Protection

Embracing the helmet of salvation involves more than acknowledging salvation; it requires actively applying its protective benefits to every aspect of your life. Here's how to fully embrace and utilize the helmet of salvation for spiritual protection:

1   **Daily Reaffirmation of Salvation**: Make it a daily practice to reaffirm your salvation and its implications for your life. Begin each day with a reminder of your secure position in Christ. This might involve reciting Scripture, praying about your identity in Christ, or meditating on the truths of salvation. By starting each day with this affirmation, you set a foundation of confidence and protection for the challenges ahead.

2   **Meditation on God's Promises**: Regularly meditate on God's promises related to salvation. This includes promises of His faithfulness, protection, and provision. Psalms 91:4 states, "He

will cover you with his pinions, and under his wings you will find refuge." By focusing on these promises, you reinforce the helmet of salvation in your mind and protect yourself from doubts and fears.

3   **Active Faith and Obedience**: Living out your faith actively and obediently reinforces the helmet of salvation. This involves aligning your actions with God's Word and seeking to live according to His will. James 1:22 encourages believers to "be doers of the word, and not hearers only." By living out your faith, you demonstrate and strengthen the protection provided by the helmet of salvation.

4   **Engaging in Spiritual Disciplines**: Engage in spiritual disciplines such as prayer, Bible study, and worship. These practices help maintain the helmet of salvation by continually renewing your mind and reinforcing your assurance of salvation. Ephesians 6:18 encourages believers to "pray at all times in the Spirit, with all prayer and supplication." Regular spiritual disciplines support your protection and growth in faith.

5   **Community Support and Accountability**: Surround yourself with a supportive Christian community that encourages and holds you accountable in your spiritual journey. Hebrews 10:24-25 emphasizes the importance of gathering together for mutual encouragement. Engaging with fellow believers provides additional protection and support for maintaining the helmet of salvation.

6   **Responding to Spiritual Attacks**: When facing spiritual attacks, consciously apply the helmet of salvation by reminding yourself of your secure position in Christ and the truth of God's promises. This proactive approach helps you stand firm against the enemy's schemes and reinforces your mental and emotional resilience.

Embracing the Helmet of Salvation: A Path to Spiritual Resilience

The helmet of salvation is a crucial component of the armor of God, providing essential protection for the mind and thoughts. This piece of spiritual armor shields you from the enemy's attempts to sow confusion, fear, and doubt. By understanding the assurance of salvation, guarding your mind, and actively embracing the helmet of salvation, you can strengthen your spiritual defense and maintain stability in the face of challenges.

Embracing the helmet of salvation involves a deep understanding of your secure position in Christ, regular reaffirmation of your salvation, and the application of spiritual disciplines. It requires immersing yourself in Scripture, prayer, and worship to reinforce your identity in Christ. By protecting your thoughts with the certainty of God's promises and living out your faith actively, you ensure that the helmet of salvation serves as a powerful shield against doubts, fears, and temptations.

As you continue to wear the helmet of salvation, you will find greater peace, confidence, and resilience in your spiritual journey. This piece of armor not only guards your mind but also fortifies your entire being, enabling you to face spiritual battles with assurance and strength. The helmet of salvation anchors your thoughts and provides clarity and protection, allowing you to withstand the trials and attacks that come your way. Embrace this vital piece of armor and experience the profound protection and victory that it brings to your life in Christ.

Moreover, the helmet of salvation is a daily reminder of the eternal hope we have in Jesus Christ. It empowers us to live with a sense of purpose and direction, knowing that our ultimate salvation is secure. This assurance not only protects our thoughts but also inspires us to live boldly and share the message of salvation with others. By embodying the peace and confidence that come with wearing the helmet of salvation, we become witnesses of God's grace and channels through which His light can shine brightly in a world in need of hope.

Chapter 6:

The Sword of the Spirit

Understanding the Word of God as a Weapon

In the spiritual armor described in Ephesians 6:10-18, the sword of the Spirit is distinguished from the other pieces by its unique function. Unlike the belt of truth, the breastplate of righteousness, or the shield of faith, the sword of the Spirit is both a defensive and offensive tool. It is described as the "Word of God," highlighting its pivotal role in spiritual warfare. Understanding the Word of God as a weapon involves recognizing its power, purpose, and application in the battles we face.

The Bible is not merely a book of religious teachings; it is a dynamic and living force with the power to transform lives and confront spiritual adversaries. Hebrews 4:12 emphasizes this: "For the word of God is alive and active, sharper than any double-edged sword; it penetrates even to dividing soul and spirit, joints and marrow; it judges the thoughts and attitudes of the heart." This verse illustrates that the Word of God is more than a guide for righteous living; it is a sharp instrument designed to cut through deception, expose sin, and empower believers to stand firm against the schemes of the enemy.

The effectiveness of the sword of the Spirit lies in its divine origin and infallible truth. Unlike earthly weapons that may become dull or ineffective over time, the Word of God remains sharp and potent. It has the power to pierce through the darkest lies, dispel the fog of confusion, and bring clarity and strength to the believer. To fully harness this weapon, it is essential to understand its role in both defense and attack.

How to Effectively Use Scripture in Spiritual Battles

Using the sword of the Spirit effectively requires more than just owning a Bible; it involves actively engaging with Scripture in ways that apply to our daily lives and spiritual battles. The process begins with knowing the Word intimately. This means not only reading the Bible but studying it deeply, memorizing key verses, and understanding its context and applications.

1. Knowing the Word:

The foundation of using Scripture effectively is a thorough knowledge of its content. This involves regular reading and study of the Bible. Familiarity with both the Old and New Testaments equips believers with a broad understanding of God's promises, principles, and character. By immersing ourselves in Scripture, we can better discern the truth and apply it to various situations.

2. Memorizing Key Verses:

Memorization is a powerful tool in spiritual warfare. When faced with temptation, doubt, or spiritual attack, having key verses readily available can provide immediate support and guidance. Verses like 1 Corinthians 10:13, which assures that God provides a way out of temptation, or James 4:7, which encourages us to resist the devil, can be crucial in moments of need.

3. Applying Scripture to Specific Situations:

The Word of God is most effective when it is applied to specific circumstances. This means using relevant scriptures to address particular challenges or temptations. For example, when dealing with anxiety, Philippians 4:6-7 provides reassurance and a prescription for prayer and peace. When confronting doubts, Romans 8:38-39 affirms the unbreakable nature of God's love.

4. Engaging in Prayer and Meditation:

Combining Scripture with prayer and meditation enhances its effectiveness. Prayer aligns our hearts with God's will and invites His power into our situation, while meditation allows us to reflect deeply on His Word and internalize its truths. Together, these practices strengthen our use of the sword of the Spirit by ensuring that our understanding and application of Scripture are rooted in a genuine relationship with God.

5. Defending Against Lies and Deception:

One of the primary functions of the sword of the Spirit is to counteract the lies and deceptions of the enemy. Jesus demonstrated this in His confrontation with Satan during His temptation in the wilderness (Matthew 4:1-11). Each time Satan tempted Him, Jesus responded with Scripture, affirming the truth and rejecting the enemy's lies. This example underscores the importance of knowing and using Scripture to defend against spiritual attacks.

Training with the Sword of the Spirit

Like any effective warrior, believers must undergo training to wield the sword of the Spirit skillfully. Training with Scripture involves consistent practice and application in various areas of life. Here are some key aspects of training with the sword of the Spirit:

1. Regular Study and Reflection:

Regularly engaging in Bible study is essential for effective training. This includes participating in personal study, group Bible studies, and listening to sound teaching from trusted leaders. Reflection on Scripture helps believers understand its implications for their lives and prepares them to use it in spiritual battles.

2. Practical Application:

Training involves applying the lessons learned from Scripture to everyday life. This means making decisions, facing challenges, and responding to situations in ways that align with biblical principles. For example, practicing forgiveness, integrity, and love according to Scripture reinforces the sword of the Spirit's role in transforming character and behavior.

3. Seeking Accountability and Guidance:

Accountability relationships with fellow believers can enhance training with the sword of the Spirit. These relationships provide opportunities for mutual encouragement, correction, and growth. Seeking guidance from mature Christians and spiritual mentors helps ensure that one's use of Scripture is sound and aligned with God's truth.

4. Cultivating a Prayerful Attitude:

Training with the sword of the Spirit is not solely about intellectual knowledge; it also involves a prayerful attitude. Prayerful engagement with Scripture invites the Holy Spirit to illuminate its meaning and application. This spiritual dimension of training ensures that the Word is not merely a tool but a living guide.

5. Practicing Spiritual Discipline:

Spiritual disciplines such as fasting, worship, and confession complement the training with the sword of the Spirit. These practices create an environment where believers are more receptive to God's Word and more capable of applying it effectively. They also help to build resilience and depth in spiritual understanding.

In summary, the sword of the Spirit, the Word of God, is a vital and powerful weapon in the believer's arsenal. By understanding its role, using it effectively in spiritual battles, and committing to ongoing training, believers can wield this sword with confidence and precision. This approach not only strengthens individual faith but also contributes to the collective victory of the body of Christ in spiritual warfare. Embrace the sword of the Spirit as a key instrument in your spiritual journey, and experience the transformative power and protection it offers.

Chapter 7:

The Power of Prayer

The Role of Prayer in Spiritual Warfare

Prayer is a cornerstone of spiritual warfare, playing a crucial role in both defense and offense against the forces of darkness. It establishes a direct line of communication between believers and God, enabling them to access divine power, wisdom, and guidance. Understanding and utilizing the power of prayer can significantly impact one's ability to navigate spiritual battles and maintain spiritual resilience.

1. A Connection to Divine Power

Prayer connects believers to the immense power of God. Through prayer, individuals tap into divine strength that surpasses human capabilities. Ephesians 6:18 instructs believers to "pray in the Spirit on all occasions with all kinds of prayers and requests." This directive highlights the need for constant and varied forms of prayer, emphasizing that prayer is not a one-time or occasional act but a continual engagement with the divine.

In spiritual warfare, accessing God's power is vital for overcoming obstacles and challenges. Prayer invites God's intervention into situations where human effort alone is insufficient. For instance, in times of crisis, prayer can bring about miraculous changes and solutions that transcend natural limitations. The effectiveness of prayer in harnessing divine power is evident in biblical accounts where prayer led to extraordinary outcomes, such as the walls of Jericho falling after the Israelites' persistent prayers and obedience (Joshua 6).

2. A Channel for God's Will

Prayer is instrumental in aligning believers with God's will. The

Lord's Prayer, found in Matthew 6:9-13, serves as a model for seeking God's will and kingdom. By praying "Your will be done," believers submit their desires and plans to God's greater purpose, ensuring that their actions are in harmony with divine intentions.

Aligning with God's will through prayer involves asking for guidance and discerning His plans for one's life. It requires humility and openness to God's direction, even when it deviates from personal expectations. By seeking God's will, believers position themselves to receive divine wisdom and direction, enabling them to navigate spiritual battles effectively.

3. A Means of Spiritual Strength

Prayer fortifies believers spiritually, providing strength and endurance in the face of adversity. The act of praying not only invokes God's power but also builds spiritual resilience. James 5:16 emphasizes that "the prayer of a righteous person is powerful and effective," underscoring the strength that prayer brings to the believer's spiritual journey.

In spiritual warfare, prayer serves as a source of empowerment and sustenance. It strengthens the believer's faith, helps maintain focus on God's promises, and fosters a sense of peace amidst turmoil. The practice of regular prayer reinforces the believer's connection with God, making it easier to withstand attacks and challenges.

Developing a Consistent Prayer Life

A consistent prayer life is foundational for leveraging the power of prayer in spiritual warfare. Developing such a routine ensures that prayer becomes a natural and integral part of daily life, providing ongoing support and strength. Here are essential steps to cultivate a consistent prayer practice:

1. Establishing a Routine

Creating a regular prayer routine is crucial for consistency.

Designating specific times each day for prayer helps establish a habit and ensures that prayer remains a priority. Morning prayers can set a positive tone for the day, while evening prayers offer a time for reflection and gratitude. Establishing a routine helps integrate prayer into daily life, making it a natural and expected part of one's schedule.

2. Setting Goals for Prayer

Setting specific goals for prayer can provide structure and motivation. Goals might include committing to a certain amount of time each day, focusing on particular topics or issues, or developing a habit of praying for others. Clear goals help maintain focus and direction, ensuring that prayer remains intentional and purposeful.

3. Using Prayer Journals

Prayer journals are valuable tools for maintaining a consistent prayer life. They offer a space to record prayer requests, track answers to prayers, and reflect on spiritual growth. Journaling provides a tangible record of God's faithfulness and helps believers see the impact of prayer over time. It also serves as a reminder of past victories and encourages continued faithfulness.

4. Incorporating Various Forms of Prayer

Incorporating different forms of prayer enriches the prayer experience. Adoration, confession, thanksgiving, and supplication each serve distinct purposes and contribute to a well-rounded prayer life. For example, adoration focuses on worshiping God for His attributes, while confession involves seeking forgiveness and reconciliation. Utilizing various forms of prayer ensures a comprehensive approach to communication with God.

5. Engaging in Corporate Prayer

Participating in corporate prayer strengthens collective faith and fosters unity. Church gatherings, prayer groups, and online communities provide platforms for shared prayer and mutual support. Corporate prayer amplifies the power of individual prayers and aligns collective efforts toward common goals. Engaging with others in prayer enhances the overall effectiveness of spiritual efforts and provides encouragement and accountability.

Utilizing Prayer as a Weapon and Defense

Prayer functions as both a weapon and a defense in spiritual warfare. Its dual role underscores its importance in both proactive and reactive strategies against spiritual adversaries.

1. Prayer as a Weapon

Using prayer as a weapon involves proactive engagement in spiritual battles. It is a strategic tool for advancing God's kingdom and confronting spiritual forces. This aspect of prayer includes several key practices:

- **Intercession:** Intercessory prayer involves standing in the gap for others, seeking God's intervention and blessings on their behalf. Interceding for individuals, communities, or nations can bring about significant spiritual change and combat the enemy's schemes. For example, praying for the salvation of loved ones or for healing in times of crisis can lead to transformative outcomes.

- **Spiritual Warfare Prayers:** Specific prayers for spiritual warfare target areas of conflict. These prayers often include declarations of God's sovereignty, rebuking of demonic influences, and requests for divine protection. Using Scripture in these prayers strengthens their impact, as the Word of God is a powerful weapon against spiritual attacks. For instance, praying passages such as Isaiah 54:17, which declares that "no weapon formed against you will prosper," reinforces faith and protection.

- **Prayers for Empowerment:** Asking for the filling of the Holy Spirit and empowerment to fulfill God's will provides believers with the authority and strength needed to face challenges. Empowering prayers help believers operate in the fullness of God's power, enabling them to confront spiritual adversaries with confidence and effectiveness.

2. Prayer as a Defense

Prayer also serves as a defensive mechanism, protecting believers from spiritual attacks and maintaining their spiritual well-being. This aspect of prayer includes:

- **Preventive Prayer:** Preventive prayer seeks God's protection and guidance to avoid potential pitfalls. By praying for wisdom, discernment, and divine intervention, believers can preemptively address potential threats and navigate challenges with greater ease. For example, praying for God's guidance before making important decisions helps avoid pitfalls and ensures alignment with His will.

- **Prayers for Peace and Strength:** In times of trial or attack, prayers for peace and strength sustain and comfort believers. These prayers focus on receiving God's peace that surpasses understanding and His strength to endure hardships. Philippians 4:6-7 encourages believers to present their requests to God, assuring them that His peace will guard their hearts and minds.

- **Prayers for Discernment:** Prayers for discernment ask for wisdom to recognize spiritual truths and deceptions. Discernment helps believers navigate complex situations and maintain clarity. For instance, praying for discernment in situations involving false teachings or spiritual deception helps believers remain steadfast in truth.

3. Building a Prayer Community

Building a community of prayer enhances the effectiveness of prayer as both a weapon and a defense. Engaging with others in prayer fosters collective strength and amplifies individual prayers. Prayer groups, church prayer teams, and online networks provide platforms for shared prayer and mutual support. By coming together in prayer, believers strengthen their spiritual resilience and encourage one another in their faith journeys.

In summary, the power of prayer in spiritual warfare is profound and multifaceted. It serves as a connection to divine power, aligns believers with God's will, and fortifies them spiritually. Developing a consistent prayer life through routine, goals, journaling, and corporate prayer ensures that prayer becomes a robust and effective tool. By utilizing prayer as both a weapon and a defense, believers can confront spiritual adversaries with confidence and resilience, drawing upon God's strength and guidance. Embracing the power of prayer equips believers to navigate spiritual warfare with greater assurance and effectiveness, ultimately leading to a more victorious and empowered life in Christ.

Chapter 8:

Standing Firm in the Strength of the Lord

Relying on God's Strength Over Your Own

In spiritual warfare, depending on God's strength rather than our own is crucial. Human strength, while valuable, is limited and prone to exhaustion. God's strength, however, is infinite and perfectly suited to every challenge. Recognizing this difference is essential for believers aiming to remain steadfast through trials.

1. The Limitations of Human Strength

Human strength is finite and often falls short in spiritual battles. Paul's words in 2 Corinthians 12:9 highlight this: "My grace is sufficient for you, for my power is made perfect in weakness." Our limitations reveal the opportunity for God's power to manifest. Reliance solely on our own strength can lead to burnout and failure, especially when facing overwhelming spiritual forces.

Practical experiences often show that human efforts can lead to stress and discouragement. In spiritual warfare, where the forces are beyond our control, recognizing our limitations prompts us to seek divine assistance. This shift from self-reliance to dependence on God is crucial for overcoming obstacles.

2. The Infinite Strength of God

God's strength contrasts sharply with human limitations. Psalm 68:35 proclaims, "You, God, are awesome in your sanctuary; the God of Israel gives power and strength to his people." God's strength is both immense and tailored to our needs. Isaiah 40:29 reassures us, "He gives strength to the weary and increases the power of the weak," emphasizing that God's strength is specific and available to address our struggles.

Relying on God means tapping into a limitless power that surpasses our capabilities. This divine strength is not generic but perfectly suited to meet individual needs. By depending on God, we align ourselves with an infinite and personal source of power.

3. Cultivating Dependence on God's Strength

Cultivating dependence on God's strength involves intentional practices and spiritual disciplines that foster a deeper connection with Him. Key practices include prayer, meditation on Scripture, and engaging with fellow believers.

Prayer connects us to God, expressing our dependence and seeking His guidance. Philippians 4:13 encapsulates this reliance: "I can do all things through Christ who strengthens me." This verse underscores that our endurance and success are rooted in Christ's empowerment.

Meditating on Scripture reinforces our reliance on God. Verses like Psalm 46:1, "God is our refuge and strength, an ever-present help in trouble," remind us of His promises. Regular meditation helps internalize these truths, integrating them into our mindset and approach to life's challenges.

Fellowship with other believers provides additional support and accountability. Community offers encouragement and shared experiences that bolster our faith. Ecclesiastes 4:9-10 highlights this: "Two are better than one... If either of them falls down, one can help the other up." Engaging with others in faith strengthens our reliance on God and offers practical assistance during difficulties.

Building Spiritual Resilience

Spiritual resilience is the ability to remain steadfast and grow in faith despite challenges. Developing this resilience involves intentional effort and commitment to practices that strengthen our faith and reliance on God.

1. Embracing Challenges as Opportunities

Seeing challenges as opportunities for growth is essential for building resilience. James 1:2-4 encourages believers to "consider it pure joy... whenever you face trials of many kinds," because trials produce perseverance. This perspective transforms adversity into a chance for spiritual development.

Facing trials with acceptance and anticipation of growth aligns us with God's purposes. Trials reveal strengths and weaknesses, offering insights into areas needing improvement. Embracing challenges with this mindset allows God to use them for our benefit, increasing resilience over time.

2. Developing Spiritual Disciplines

Spiritual disciplines, such as prayer, fasting, Bible study, worship, and service, are vital for growth and resilience. Each practice contributes to a deeper relationship with God and enhances our ability to withstand challenges.

- **Prayer:** Regular, heartfelt prayer maintains our connection to God, reinforcing our dependence on His strength. It provides a platform for expressing concerns and seeking guidance.

- **Fasting:** Fasting, which involves abstaining from food or comforts to focus on spiritual matters, enhances sensitivity to God's voice and strengthens our resolve to seek Him above all else.

- **Bible Study:** Engaging with Scripture deepens our understanding of God's promises and teachings, offering guidance and encouragement to handle challenges effectively.

- **Worship:** Worship centers our focus on God's greatness and goodness, renewing our perspective and reminding us of His power and faithfulness.

- **Service:** Serving others aligns us with God's purposes and fosters a sense of purpose. It also builds resilience by shifting focus from personal problems to the needs of others.

3. Building a Support Network

A supportive faith community is crucial for resilience. Engaging with a network of believers provides encouragement, accountability, and shared wisdom. Hebrews 10:24-25 encourages believers to "spur one another on toward love and good deeds," and to meet regularly for mutual support.

Such a network offers practical assistance and emotional support during challenges. Building and nurturing relationships within a faith community creates a foundation of support that reinforces spiritual resilience.

Encouragement and Strategies for Standing Firm

Standing firm in the strength of the Lord requires practical strategies and encouragement. Here are key strategies and sources of encouragement for maintaining resilience:

1. Daily Affirmations of Faith

Affirming faith daily reinforces reliance on God's strength. Personal declarations and Scripture reminders, like Romans 8:37, "in all these things we are more than conquerors through him who loved us," bolster confidence in God's power.

2. Setting Spiritual Goals

Spiritual goals, such as regular prayer or Bible reading, provide focus and motivation. These goals help align efforts with the commitment to standing firm in faith.

3. Reflecting on Past Victories

Reflecting on past experiences where God's strength was evident builds confidence. Remembering how God has delivered and sustained us reinforces trust in His future provision. Psalm 77:11-12 encourages us to "remember the deeds of the Lord; yes, I will remember your miracles of long ago."

4. Seeking Ongoing Training

Ongoing training through Bible studies, workshops, and discipleship programs equips us to handle challenges effectively. This continual growth reinforces our faith and reliance on God.

5. Maintaining a Heart of Gratitude

Cultivating gratitude shifts focus from problems to blessings. 1 Thessalonians 5:18 instructs us to "give thanks in all circumstances," fostering a positive perspective and reinforcing trust in God's care.

Conclusion: Embracing Divine Strength

Standing firm in the strength of the Lord is vital for spiritual resilience and effective spiritual warfare. By relying on God's limitless power, we overcome obstacles and maintain unwavering faith. Building resilience involves embracing challenges, developing spiritual disciplines, and nurturing a supportive community. Through daily affirmations, setting goals, reflecting on victories, seeking training, and cultivating gratitude, believers reinforce their reliance on divine strength. Embracing these practices equips us to face challenges with confidence and perseverance, experiencing the transformative power of God's strength in our lives.

Chapter 9:

Preparing for Specific Battles

Identifying and Preparing for Personal Spiritual Challenges

In the journey of faith, every believer faces unique spiritual challenges that require intentional preparation and strategy. Identifying these challenges is the first step in preparing for specific battles. Just as a soldier must know the terrain and the enemy before engaging in combat, a Christian must recognize the particular areas where they are most vulnerable to spiritual attacks.

1. Self-Reflection and Prayerful Examination

To identify personal spiritual challenges, it's crucial to engage in self-reflection and prayerful examination. This involves taking time to assess your spiritual strengths and weaknesses. Ask yourself questions like: Where am I most tempted? What areas of my life are under the most spiritual attack? Which sins do I struggle with repeatedly?

Prayer plays a vital role in this process. By seeking God's guidance through prayer, you can gain insight into the specific areas of your life that need attention. Psalm 139:23-24 is a powerful scripture to meditate on during this time: "Search me, God, and know my heart; test me and know my anxious thoughts. See if there is any offensive way in me and lead me in the way everlasting." Through prayer, God can reveal hidden weaknesses and areas where the enemy may be targeting you.

2. Understanding Common Spiritual Battles

While every believer's spiritual challenges are unique, some battles are common across the Christian experience. These include struggles with doubt, fear, pride, anger, and temptation. Understanding these common battles can help you prepare more effectively.

For instance, doubt often arises during times of crisis or uncertainty. Knowing this, you can proactively fortify your faith by immersing yourself in God's promises and surrounding yourself with a supportive community of believers. Similarly, fear can be countered by meditating on scriptures that affirm God's protection and love, such as Isaiah 41:10: "So do not fear, for I am with you; do not be dismayed, for I am your God. I will strengthen you and help you; I will uphold you with my righteous right hand."

3. Developing a Battle Plan

Once you've identified your specific spiritual challenges, the next step is to develop a battle plan. This plan should include strategies for strengthening your spiritual armor, as described in Ephesians 6:10-18. Each piece of the armor of God plays a vital role in defending against spiritual attacks.

For example, if you struggle with doubt, focus on strengthening the "shield of faith" by immersing yourself in the Word of God, which builds and sustains faith (Romans 10:17). If temptation is your primary challenge, ensure that your "sword of the Spirit," which is the Word of God, is sharp and ready for use. This means memorizing scriptures that speak directly to your areas of temptation, enabling you to counter the enemy's lies with truth.

Tailoring your armor involves applying the principles of the armor of God to your specific situation. For instance, the "helmet of salvation" protects your mind from doubts and fears by reminding you of your secure position in Christ. Regularly affirming your identity in Christ can help you stand firm in the face of attacks on your self-worth or assurance of salvation.

Tailoring Your Armor for Various Situations

Spiritual warfare is not a one-size-fits-all battle. Different situations require different strategies, and the armor of God must be tailored accordingly. Tailoring your armor involves understanding how each piece of armor applies to specific challenges and situations.

1. The Belt of Truth

The belt of truth is foundational for every spiritual battle, as it represents the truth of God's Word that holds everything together. In situations where you are confronted with deception or false teachings, the belt of truth is your primary defense. By grounding yourself in the truth of Scripture, you can discern lies and stand firm against the enemy's attempts to deceive you.

2. The Breastplate of Righteousness

The breastplate of righteousness protects your heart and soul from the enemy's attacks on your character and integrity. In situations where you face accusations, guilt, or shame, the breastplate of righteousness reminds you of your righteousness in Christ. This righteousness is not earned by works but is a gift from God through faith (Philippians 3:9). By living a life of integrity and obedience to God, you keep your breastplate secure, guarding your heart against the enemy's arrows.

3. The Shoes of the Gospel of Peace

The shoes of the gospel of peace equip you to stand firm and move forward in the midst of conflict and uncertainty. In situations where you encounter chaos, fear, or relational strife, the peace of God acts as both a stabilizer and a guide. Philippians 4:7 promises that "the peace of God, which transcends all understanding, will guard your hearts and your minds in Christ Jesus." By keeping your focus on the gospel and walking in peace, you can navigate difficult situations with confidence and poise.

4. The Shield of Faith

The shield of faith is essential in situations where you are under direct spiritual attack. Faith is your defense against the fiery darts of the enemy, which can come in the form of doubt, fear, and discouragement. To tailor your shield of faith, immerse yourself in God's promises and remind yourself of His faithfulness. Faith is not just belief but trust in action. By actively trusting in God's character and His Word, you can extinguish the enemy's fiery darts and stand firm.

5. The Helmet of Salvation

The helmet of salvation guards your mind against doubts and fears, reminding you of your secure position in Christ. In situations where your faith is challenged or you face uncertainty about your salvation, the helmet of salvation is your protection. By regularly affirming your identity in Christ and the assurance of your salvation, you can keep your mind focused on the hope and security that comes from knowing you are saved.

6. The Sword of the Spirit

The sword of the Spirit, which is the Word of God, is both an offensive and defensive weapon. In situations where you need to confront lies, temptation, or spiritual opposition, the sword of the Spirit is your primary weapon. To tailor your sword, memorize and meditate on scriptures that address your specific challenges. The more familiar you are with God's Word, the more effectively you can wield it in battle.

Case Studies and Testimonies

Real-life examples and testimonies of how others have prepared for and overcome specific spiritual battles can provide valuable insights and encouragement. By learning from the experiences of others, you can gain practical strategies for your own spiritual warfare.

1. Overcoming Doubt and Fear

Sarah, a young woman struggling with doubt and fear, found herself questioning her faith during a difficult season of life. She was overwhelmed by anxiety and uncertainty about her future. To prepare for this battle, Sarah immersed herself in the Word of God, particularly focusing on scriptures that spoke to God's faithfulness and sovereignty. She also surrounded herself with a supportive community of believers who encouraged her and prayed with her. By tailoring her armor with the shield of faith and the helmet of salvation, Sarah was able to stand firm and overcome her doubts and fears.

2. Battling Temptation

John, a man struggling with addiction, faced a constant battle with temptation. He knew that his human strength was not enough to overcome the powerful pull of his addiction. To prepare for this battle, John tailored his armor by memorizing scriptures that spoke to God's power to deliver and heal. He also engaged in regular prayer and fasting, seeking God's strength to resist temptation. By wielding the sword of the Spirit and relying on the strength of God, John was able to experience victory over his addiction.

3. Standing Firm in Faith During Persecution

Maria, a believer living in a country hostile to Christianity, faced persecution for her faith. She knew that standing firm in her faith would come at a great personal cost. To prepare for this battle, Maria tailored her armor by deepening her understanding of the gospel and regularly affirming her identity in Christ. She also connected with a small group of believers who provided support and encouragement. By putting on the breastplate of righteousness and the shoes of the gospel of peace, Maria was able to stand firm in her faith despite the persecution she faced.

4. Resisting the Lure of Pride

David, a successful businessman, found himself battling the lure of pride as his career flourished. He realized that his achievements were leading him to rely more on his abilities than on God. To prepare for this battle, David tailored his armor by focusing on humility and service. He regularly meditated on scriptures that emphasized the importance of humility, such as Philippians 2:3-4: "Do nothing out of selfish ambition or vain conceit. Rather, in humility value others above yourselves, not looking to your own interests but each of you to the interests of the others." By putting on the belt of truth and the breastplate of righteousness, David was able to resist the lure of pride and maintain a humble heart.

5. Fighting Discouragement in Ministry

Rachel, a pastor's wife, faced discouragement in ministry as she dealt with the challenges of leading a congregation. The weight of responsibility and the criticisms she received left her feeling weary and disheartened. To prepare for this battle, Rachel tailored her armor by focusing on the joy of the Lord as her strength (Nehemiah 8:10). She also made time for personal prayer and worship, allowing God to refresh her spirit. By wielding the shield of faith and the sword of the Spirit, Rachel was able to fight discouragement and continue serving with a renewed sense of purpose.

Applying Lessons Learned

The case studies and testimonies of others provide valuable lessons for our own spiritual battles. Whether facing doubt, temptation, persecution, pride, or discouragement, the key to victory lies in identifying your specific challenges, tailoring your armor, and relying on God's strength. By learning from the experiences of others and applying these principles to your own life, you can prepare for and overcome the specific battles you face.

Conclusion: Staying Vigilant in the Battle

Spiritual warfare is an ongoing reality for every believer. The enemy is relentless, but so is the power and grace of God. As you prepare for specific battles, remember that your strength comes from the Lord (Ephesians 6:10). Stay vigilant, keep your armor tailored and ready, and trust in God's unfailing power to give you victory in every situation.

In the words of 2 Corinthians 10:4-5, "The weapons we fight with are not the weapons of the world. On the contrary, they have divine power to demolish strongholds. We demolish arguments and every pretension that sets itself up against the knowledge of God, and we take captive every thought to make it obedient to Christ." May you be equipped, empowered, and encouraged as you face the specific battles in your life, knowing that victory is assured in Christ.

Chapter 10:

Maintaining Your Armor

The Importance of Regular Spiritual Maintenance

Maintaining your spiritual armor is crucial for effectively engaging in spiritual warfare and ensuring ongoing protection against the forces of darkness. Just as a soldier must regularly maintain their physical armor to ensure its effectiveness in battle, believers must engage in regular spiritual maintenance to keep their spiritual armor in top condition. This chapter explores why regular spiritual maintenance is vital, how to practice it, and how to ensure continuous growth and readiness in your spiritual journey.

1. Understanding the Need for Spiritual Maintenance

The concept of spiritual maintenance is rooted in the need for ongoing vigilance and care in our walk with God. Spiritual armor, as described in Ephesians 6:10-18, includes elements like the belt of truth, breastplate of righteousness, shoes of peace, shield of faith, helmet of salvation, and sword of the Spirit. Each piece represents a critical aspect of our spiritual life and protection. Just as physical armor can wear down, become damaged, or become less effective over time without proper care, so too can our spiritual armor if not maintained regularly.

The importance of spiritual maintenance lies in its role in preserving our effectiveness in spiritual battles and our overall spiritual health. Regular maintenance helps us remain strong in our faith, equipped to handle challenges, and resilient in the face of spiritual attacks. Without it, we risk becoming vulnerable to deception, discouragement, and defeat.

2. The Consequences of Neglect

Neglecting spiritual maintenance can have serious consequences for our spiritual well-being and effectiveness. Just as a soldier who neglects their armor might suffer injuries or defeat, a believer who neglects their spiritual armor may experience spiritual vulnerability and defeat. This neglect can manifest in various ways:

- **Spiritual Weakness:** Without regular maintenance, our spiritual armor can become ineffective, leading to a weakened defense against spiritual attacks. This weakness can leave us more susceptible to temptation, doubt, and discouragement.

- **Loss of Spiritual Vitality:** Regular spiritual practices like prayer, Bible study, and worship are essential for maintaining a vibrant and active faith. Neglecting these practices can result in spiritual stagnation, a lack of growth, and a diminished sense of connection with God.

- **Increased Vulnerability to Deception:** Spiritual neglect can make us more susceptible to deception and false teachings. Without ongoing engagement with Scripture and spiritual disciplines, we may be more easily led astray by erroneous beliefs or worldly influences.

- **Reduced Effectiveness in Spiritual Warfare:** Our ability to effectively combat spiritual forces relies on the strength and effectiveness of our spiritual armor. Neglecting maintenance can hinder our effectiveness in prayer, witnessing, and other aspects of spiritual warfare.

3. The Role of Regular Maintenance in Spiritual Health

Regular maintenance plays a critical role in sustaining our spiritual health and effectiveness. It ensures that our spiritual armor remains strong, effective, and ready for battle. This ongoing care involves several key practices:

- **Daily Prayer:** Prayer is essential for maintaining a strong connection with God and ensuring our spiritual armor remains effective. Through prayer, we seek God's guidance, express our needs, and receive strength and encouragement. Regular, heartfelt prayer helps us stay attuned to God's will and equipped to face challenges.

- **Consistent Bible Study:** Engaging with Scripture is vital for maintaining the truth in our lives and reinforcing our understanding of God's promises and commands. Regular Bible study keeps our spiritual armor aligned with God's Word and helps us recognize and counteract deception.

- **Worship and Praise:** Worship is a powerful practice that renews our focus on God's greatness and goodness. Regular worship and praise help strengthen our faith, reinforce our spiritual armor, and maintain a positive, resilient attitude.

- **Fellowship and Accountability:** Engaging with a community of believers provides support, encouragement, and accountability. Regular fellowship helps us stay connected, receive wisdom and guidance, and maintain our spiritual readiness.

- **Self-Examination and Reflection:** Regular self-examination allows us to assess the condition of our spiritual armor and identify areas needing improvement. Reflection on our spiritual life helps us recognize weaknesses, address issues, and make necessary adjustments.

Practices for Keeping Your Armor in Good Condition

Maintaining the effectiveness of your spiritual armor requires intentional practices and a commitment to spiritual growth. Here are some practical steps to ensure your armor remains in good condition:

1. Routine Spiritual Check-Ups

Just as physical armor requires regular inspections and repairs, our spiritual armor needs routine check-ups to ensure its effectiveness. Schedule regular times for self-examination and reflection on your spiritual life. Assess your prayer life, Bible study habits, and overall spiritual health. Identify areas where you may be struggling or where your armor may need strengthening.

2. Engaging in Spiritual Disciplines

Spiritual disciplines are practices that nurture and strengthen our faith. Incorporate key disciplines into your daily routine to keep your spiritual armor in top condition:

- **Daily Devotions:** Set aside time each day for personal devotions, including reading Scripture, praying, and meditating on God's Word. This daily practice helps reinforce your spiritual armor and keep your faith vibrant.

- **Fasting and Prayer:** Periodically engage in fasting and prayer to deepen your spiritual connection and strengthen your resolve. Fasting helps sharpen your focus on God and enhances your sensitivity to His guidance.

- **Scripture Memorization:** Memorize key Bible verses that reinforce the truth and promises of God. This practice helps internalize Scripture, making it readily available for use in spiritual battles.

- **Worship and Praise:** Regularly participate in worship and praise, both individually and with others. Worship renews your perspective and reinforces your reliance on God's strength and grace.

3. Regular Fellowship and Community Engagement

Maintain regular involvement in a faith community to receive support, encouragement, and accountability. Engage in group Bible studies, prayer meetings, and other church activities to stay connected with fellow believers. Community involvement helps reinforce your spiritual armor and provides practical assistance in times of need.

4. Addressing and Overcoming Weaknesses

Identify and address any weaknesses in your spiritual armor. If you notice areas where you struggle, such as doubt, temptation, or spiritual lethargy, take proactive steps to address them. Seek guidance from spiritual mentors, engage in specific prayer and study, and apply practical strategies to overcome challenges.

5. Seeking Continuous Growth

Continuous growth is essential for maintaining the effectiveness of your spiritual armor. Pursue opportunities for learning and development in your faith journey:

- **Attend Spiritual Training:** Participate in seminars, workshops, and conferences that provide spiritual training and growth opportunities. These events offer valuable insights and practical tools for strengthening your faith.

- **Engage in Discipleship:** Seek out discipleship programs or mentors who can provide guidance and support in your spiritual growth. Engaging in discipleship helps you deepen your understanding of God's Word and strengthen your spiritual practices.

- **Read Christian Literature:** Explore books, articles, and other resources that provide spiritual insights and encouragement. Reading Christian literature can offer new perspectives, practical advice, and inspiration for maintaining and strengthening your spiritual armor.

Continuous Growth and Readiness

Maintaining your spiritual armor involves a commitment to continuous growth and readiness. Here are some strategies to ensure you remain equipped and prepared for spiritual battles:

1. Set Spiritual Goals

Establish clear spiritual goals to guide your growth and maintenance efforts. Goals might include specific areas of improvement, such as deepening your prayer life, increasing your Bible study time, or developing a particular spiritual discipline. Setting goals provides direction and motivation for ongoing growth.

2. Stay Vigilant and Alert

Maintain a vigilant and alert mindset in your spiritual journey. Recognize that spiritual challenges and attacks can arise at any time. Stay prepared by regularly engaging in spiritual practices, staying connected with God, and remaining open to His guidance.

3. Foster a Resilient Mindset

Develop a resilient mindset that embraces challenges and remains steadfast in faith. Cultivate an attitude of perseverance and trust in God's strength. Remember that spiritual growth often involves overcoming obstacles and facing difficulties with courage and faith.

4. Seek Regular Feedback and Accountability

Regularly seek feedback and accountability from trusted spiritual mentors, friends, or group members. Share your struggles, progress, and prayer requests with others who can provide support, encouragement, and constructive feedback.

5. Embrace God's Grace and Strength

Finally, embrace God's grace and strength as you maintain your spiritual armor. Recognize that your efforts are supported by God's power and grace. Lean on His strength and trust in His promises as you continue to grow and prepare for spiritual battles.

Conclusion

Maintaining your spiritual armor is an ongoing process that requires intentional effort, commitment, and regular care. By understanding the importance of spiritual maintenance, practicing key disciplines, and pursuing continuous growth, you can ensure that your armor remains strong and effective. Regular check-ups, active engagement in spiritual practices, and a commitment to growth and readiness are essential for standing firm in your faith and effectively navigating spiritual challenges.

As you continue to invest in the maintenance of your spiritual armor, you will experience increased strength, resilience, and readiness for the spiritual battles that lie ahead. Embrace this ongoing journey with dedication and trust in God's provision and grace. By maintaining your spiritual armor, you fortify your ability to stand firm, overcome obstacles, and live a victorious life in Christ.

Conclusion:

A Life of Preparedness and Victory

Embracing a Lifestyle of Spiritual Readiness

Living a life of spiritual preparedness involves more than occasional engagement with faith; it is about embracing a continuous lifestyle of readiness and vigilance. Spiritual readiness requires adopting practices and mindsets that enable us to effectively navigate the challenges and opportunities of our faith journey. This lifestyle of preparedness ensures that we are always equipped to face spiritual battles and to live victoriously in Christ.

1. The Call to Continuous Readiness

The call to spiritual readiness is a call to live each day with an awareness of our spiritual environment and an understanding of the ongoing battle between good and evil. This readiness involves maintaining a proactive stance in our spiritual lives, engaging regularly in practices that fortify our faith and keep us attuned to God's guidance.

To embrace this lifestyle, we must first recognize that spiritual readiness is not a one-time achievement but a continuous process. It requires daily commitment to prayer, Bible study, worship, and other spiritual disciplines. By cultivating these habits, we create a foundation that supports our spiritual growth and equips us for the challenges we encounter.

2. Building Spiritual Resilience

Part of living a life of preparedness is building spiritual resilience. Resilience is the ability to bounce back from adversity and to remain steadfast in faith despite difficulties. This resilience is developed through regular engagement with spiritual practices, the support of a faith community, and a personal relationship with God.

Resilient believers are those who have learned to rely on God's strength, embrace His promises, and remain steadfast in their commitment to Him. Building resilience involves facing trials with a positive attitude, viewing challenges as opportunities for growth, and maintaining a focus on God's provision and faithfulness.

3. Cultivating a Spirit of Vigilance

Vigilance is a key component of spiritual readiness. It means being alert to spiritual dangers, aware of potential pitfalls, and proactive in addressing any areas of weakness. Cultivating vigilance involves regular self-examination, staying informed about spiritual trends, and seeking guidance from trusted mentors.

To remain vigilant, it is important to be proactive in identifying and addressing areas where we might be vulnerable. This includes recognizing and resisting temptation, avoiding negative influences, and actively seeking to grow in areas where we may be weak.

Living in Victory through the Armor of God

Living in victory is the ultimate goal of embracing a lifestyle of spiritual readiness. The armor of God, as described in Ephesians 6:10-18, provides the essential components for living a victorious Christian life. Each piece of the armor—truth, righteousness, peace, faith, salvation, and the Word of God—plays a vital role in our ability to overcome challenges and live out our faith.

1. Walking in the Fullness of God's Armor

To live in victory, it is essential to walk in the fullness of God's armor. This means not only understanding the components of the armor but also actively applying them in our daily lives. Each piece of the armor represents a vital aspect of our spiritual defense and offense.

- **The Belt of Truth:** Embrace and uphold God's truth in all areas of your life. Let truth guide your actions, decisions, and interactions with others.
- **The Breastplate of Righteousness:** Strive to live a life of righteousness, reflecting God's character in your thoughts, words, and deeds.
- **The Shoes of Peace:** Walk in the peace that comes from knowing and trusting God. Allow His peace to guide you in your relationships and decisions.
- **The Shield of Faith:** Use your faith as a shield to protect against doubts, fears, and attacks. Trust in God's promises and His ability to protect and provide.
- **The Helmet of Salvation:** Remember your salvation and the hope it brings. Let the assurance of your salvation protect your mind from discouragement and confusion.

- **The Sword of the Spirit:** Engage with Scripture as your primary tool for spiritual growth and defense. Use the Word of God to counteract lies and to strengthen your faith.

2. Experiencing Daily Victory

Living in victory is not just about momentary success but about experiencing daily triumphs in our spiritual lives. This involves consistently applying the armor of God, relying on His strength, and maintaining a positive outlook even in the face of challenges.

Daily victory is experienced through:

- **Consistent Application:** Apply the principles of the armor of God in your daily life. Make a conscious effort to live out these principles in your interactions, decisions, and responses to challenges.
- **Trusting in God's Provision:** Trust in God's ability to provide for your needs and to guide you through difficulties. Maintain a posture of faith and dependence on His strength and wisdom.
- **Celebrating Small Victories:** Recognize and celebrate the small victories in your spiritual journey. Each step forward is a testament to God's faithfulness and your growth in faith.

3. Living as a Testimony of Victory

Living in victory also involves being a testimony of God's power and grace. Your life can serve as a witness to others of what it means to walk in faith and to overcome challenges through the armor of God.

By living authentically and demonstrating the impact of your faith, you can inspire others to seek God and to embrace the victory available to them. Share your experiences, offer encouragement, and be a source of hope for those around you.

Final Encouragement and Reflections

As we conclude this journey through the armor of God and the principles of spiritual readiness, it is important to reflect on the significance of these practices and their impact on our lives. Embracing a lifestyle of preparedness and living in victory are not just ideals but practical realities that can transform our daily experiences and our relationship with God.

1. Embrace the Journey

Embrace the journey of spiritual growth with a sense of purpose and commitment. Recognize that spiritual readiness and victory are ongoing processes that require dedication and effort. Stay committed to your spiritual practices, remain vigilant, and continue to grow in your faith.

2. Trust in God's Faithfulness

Trust in God's faithfulness to guide and sustain you. He has equipped you with the armor of God and has promised to be with you in every challenge. Lean on His strength, seek His guidance, and trust in His ability to provide for all your needs.

3. Encourage Others

As you experience victory in your own life, use your testimony to encourage and uplift others. Share the lessons you've learned, offer support and prayer, and be a source of hope for those who may be struggling. Your journey can inspire others to pursue their own path of spiritual readiness and victory.

4. Remain Hopeful and Expectant

Remain hopeful and expectant for the future. God has great plans for your life and has promised to work all things together for your good. Embrace each day with a sense of anticipation, knowing that God is at work in your life and is leading you toward greater growth and victory.

5. Celebrate Your Progress

Finally, celebrate the progress you have made in your spiritual journey. Acknowledge the ways in which you have grown, the victories you have achieved, and the ways in which God has worked in your life. Take time to thank God for His faithfulness and to rejoice in the blessings He has provided.

In conclusion, a life of preparedness and victory is achievable through a commitment to spiritual readiness, the effective use of the armor of God, and a dedication to continuous growth. Embrace this lifestyle with enthusiasm, trust in God's guidance, and live each day with confidence and hope. By doing so, you will experience the fullness of God's promises and live a victorious life in Christ.

NOTES

NOTES

NOTES

NOTES

NOTES

NOTES

Made in the USA
Columbia, SC
19 October 2024

44420008R00039